EXPERIMENTS with AIR

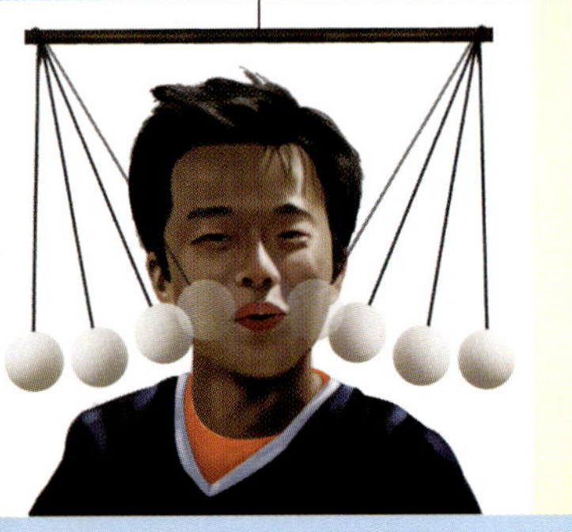

Contents

Air Is All Around

Air is everywhere. It fills space all around us. It forms the atmosphere in which we live and is held around the surface of the earth by the earth's gravity. We breathe air, but cannot see, smell or taste it. That is why we often forget that it is there. The best way to learn about air is to check what it does.

How empty is an empty bottle?

You will need:

- a bowl of water
- a bottle with a narrow neck
- some tissue paper

1. Thrust the narrow-necked bottle, mouth down, into the bowl of water.
2. Slowly tilt the bottle towards the surface of the water. What do you find? Was the bottle really empty?
3. Wipe the bottle dry. Squeeze the tissue paper into the bottom of the bottle and repeat step one.
4. Lift the bottle. What keeps the paper dry?

Find out

Take a lump of soil and a glass of water.
Can you show that the soil has air?

Fill a bottle with air

You will need:

- a bowl of water
- a bottle
- a flexible straw
- some food colouring

1. Stir the food colouring into the bowl of water.
2. Lower the mouth of the bottle into the bowl so that it fills up with the coloured water. The bottle is now upside down in the bowl.
3. Lift the bottle so that the rim of the bottle is under water. The air pressing down on the surface of the water in the bowl will stop the water in the bottle from running out.
4. Tilt the bottle slightly, and, using the flexible straw, gently blow in air through the straw.

What do you observe?

The bottle slowly fills with air.

Can you fill this bottle with water?

1. Take a funnel and place it in the neck of a bottle.
2. Secure the funnel tightly to the bottle with plasticine.
3. Can you fill the bottle with water by pouring water into the funnel? Why not?
4. Can you, if you are given a nail?

(Hint: Make a hole through the plasticine into the inside of the bottle.)

What Is Air Made Of?

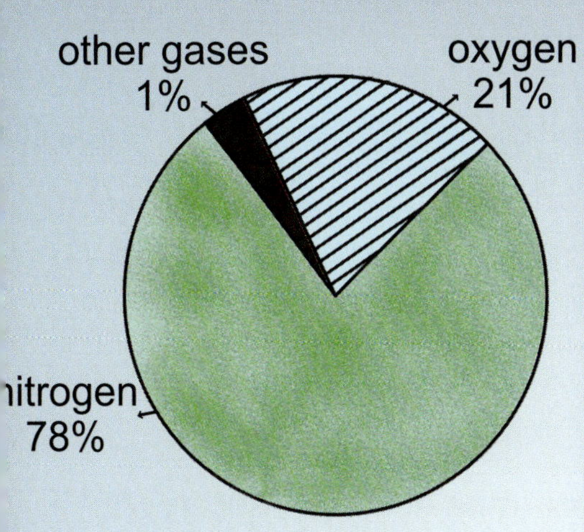

Air is an invisible mixture of gases, consisting mainly of oxygen and nitrogen. The picture on the left shows the composition of air.

The oxygen in the air keeps us alive. When we breathe in, air is sucked into our lungs, and oxygen passes into the blood. The blood carries oxygen to every part of the body. This oxygen is needed to release the energy stored in the food we eat.

Plants and animals need oxygen too.

Feel your pulse

1. Gently press your thumb or two fingers on the inside of your wrist. You will feel a beat. This is your pulse. It tells you how fast your heart is beating.
2. Count your heartbeats for a minute. They will be around 72.
3. Now, run for a minute and count again.
   What causes the count to increase?

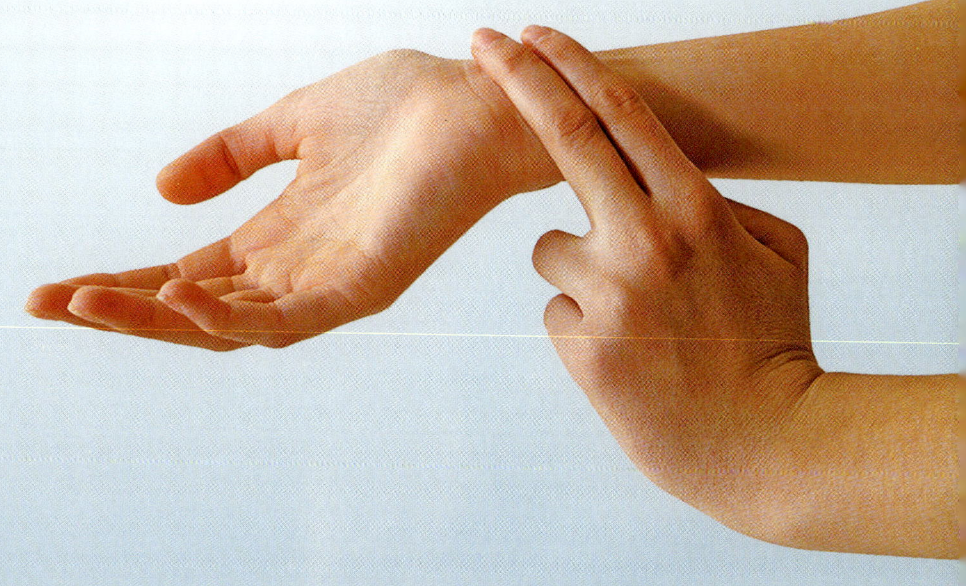

Lung capacity

You will need:

- a bathtub
- a plastic tube and a ruler
- a large bottle
- a measuring cylinder or jug
- friends

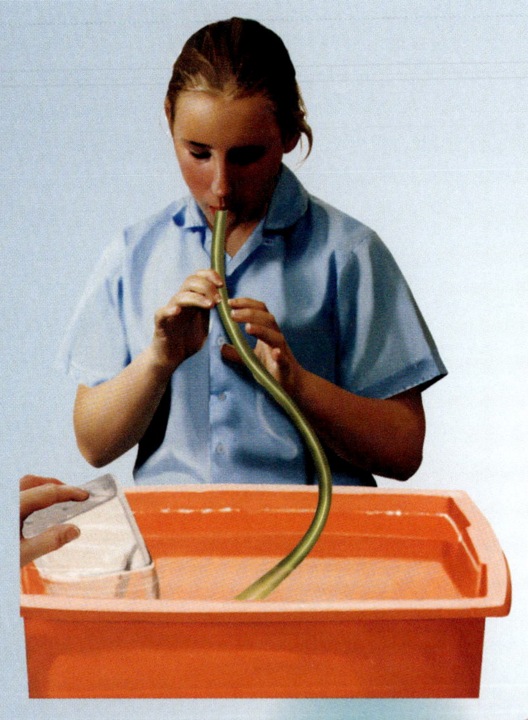

1. Fill the bathtub with water.
2. Tie the ruler to the bottle and fill it with water.
3. Cover the neck of the bottle with your hand and carefully overturn it into the tub.
4. Ask a friend to keep the bottle vertical. Note the water level reading on the ruler.
5. Pass the tube into the neck of the bottle.
6. Take a deep breath and blow hard into the tubing.
7. Mark the water level when you have finished.
8. Turn the bottle up the right way again. Using the measuring jug, pour the water so as to fill the bottle up to the first reading. The amount of water you add is roughly the same as the amount of air in your lungs. It is called your *lung capacity*.
9. Check the lung capacity of your friends.

For each lungful of fresh air we breathe in, what do we breathe out? We expel carbon dioxide (CO_2) with every breath. Carbon dioxide is harmful. That is why the presence of too many people in a small room makes you feel suffocated.

Exhaled air contains CO_2

You will need:

- two flasks with two-holed stoppers
- two straight glass tubes
- a T-shaped glass tube, as shown in the figure
- slaked lime
- water
- a bowl

1. In a bowl, mix the slaked lime with water and keep it for some hours. Strain the clear water. This is lime water.
2. Pour the lime water into the two flasks.
3. Connect the tubes to the flasks as shown in the figure. Make sure that the long tubes are inside the lime water.
4. Breathe through the T piece, closing the tube of flask two with your finger when you breathe in air, and closing the tube of flask one as you breathe out. After some time, you will notice that the lime water in the second flask has turned milky, due to CO_2 in the expelled air.

Note the direction of arrows in the figure to understand the flow of air.

Things need oxygen to burn

You will need:

- 4 candles
- 4 saucers
- 4 glass jars of different sizes
- a matchbox

1. Fix the candles on the saucers.
2. Light the candles.
3. Invert the jars over the burning candles.

How long do they burn? You will find that the candle in the smallest jar is the first to go out because the supply of air in it was the least.

A chemical process, like burning, in which things combine with oxygen, is called *oxidation*.

Oxidation occurs in nature

You must have noticed how fruits which have been cut for a while change colour when kept uncovered.

Find out

Slice some fruits into two bowls. Squeeze some lemon juice into one of the bowls. Cover it and keep it in the refrigerator. Leave the other bowl out in the air. Check the fruits after an hour. Which one has turned brown?

Rust

When iron is left in water or damp air, it reacts with the oxygen in the air to form a red powder, which we call *rust*. You can check this easily.

You will need:

- a test-tube or a narrow medicine bottle
- a small wad of steel wool
- a beaker
- water

1. Place the steel wool in the test-tube.
2. Fill the beaker with water and invert the test-tube in the water, as shown in the picture. Keep it for 24 hours.
3. Look at the test-tube. What do you observe? Has the steel wool changed colour? Is there any change in the level of water in the test-tube? How do you account for this?

What else does air contain?

Apart from the gases we have talked about, air has carbon and other dust particles, and spores of fungi floating in it. Have you seen bluish-green moulds formed on stale bread and cheese? Moulds form when the spores in the air land on food and get the right environment and temperature to produce more spores.

Air Has Weight

Weight is the force by which all things are pulled towards the earth by gravity. Air, like everything else, is also pulled by gravity and must have weight. But as air is very light, it is difficult to show that it has weight. However, let us try.

You will need:

- a metre stick
- thread
- two bulldog clips
- two balloons

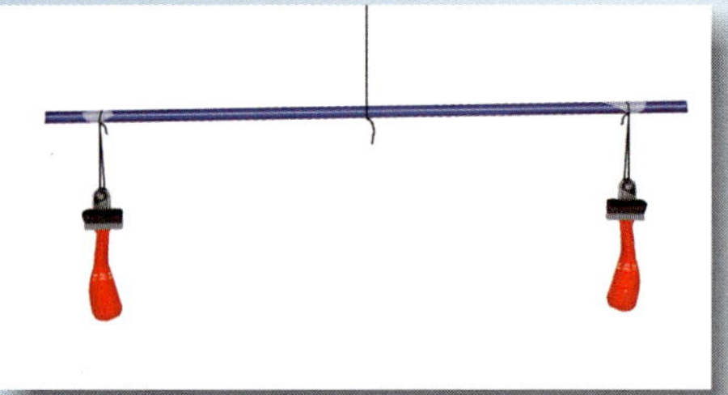

1. Hang the stick at its mid-point by a piece of thread.
2. Hang the bulldog clips at the two ends of the stick and attach the balloons, as shown in the picture.
3. Slide the clips to obtain a balance.
4. Ask a friend to hold the stick while you carefully remove one balloon and blow it up.
5. Tie the balloon at its neck and hang it back in its place.
6. Check what happens when your friend lets go of the balance.

[Remember: Blow the balloon very hard for good results. An increase in the volume of the balloon will increase the upward thrust of air displaced by it.]

As light as air

You will surely hesitate to use this phrase, once you are aware that the total weight of the earth's atmosphere is one million billion tonnes. A column of the atmosphere one square inch and 600 miles high weighs nearly 15 pounds. This means that the atmosphere presses every inch of you with a weight of nearly 15 lbs (Ouch!).

But then why does this great pressure not crush us? It is thanks to the air that enters our body through the mouth and nose, and the air in the body cells that pushes outward with an opposing pressure.

Warm air is lighter than cold air

When air is heated, it expands, or gets bigger in volume. You can check this easily.

1. Tie a small balloon over the neck of a small bottle.
2. Place the bottle in a pan of warm water.
3. What do you find? The balloon blows up because the air in the bottle gets heated and expands.

The particles of warm air move further apart and take up more space. It becomes less dense and lighter. This causes warm air to rise above the colder, heavier air.

Have you seen hot air balloons floating in the sky? A hot air balloon is heated by a gas flame below the balloon. The hot air inside the balloon being lighter than the cooler surrounding air, forces it to rise. When the gas flame is turned down, the air cools and the balloon sinks back to the ground.

Which is lighter?

You will need:

- a yardstick or a metre rule
- a long thin nail
- two drinking glasses
- two paper bags of the same size
- thread
- a candle
- a matchbox

1. Drive the nail through the exact centre of the stick.
2. Balance the stick by resting the nail on the rims of the two glasses. Get an exact balance.
3. Cut two lengths of thread, 20 cm each. Tie a knot at one end of each thread and insert them through the bottom of the bags. Make loops at the other end that will go over the balance rod.
4. Place a bag at each end of the rod. Move the bags in or out until they are in exact balance.
5. Light a candle and hold it well below one of the bags so as to heat the air for several minutes.

What do you find? What can you say from this?

Hot air fans

1. Take some coloured paper or tin foil and cut them into discs.
2. Draw a smaller circle inside each disc. Divide the discs into eight segments and cut along the segments up to the smaller circles.
3. Bend the edges as shown in the figure.
4. Tie them to a rod with threads of varying length.
5. Hang it over the hot air rising from a radiator or a candle flame.
6. Watch the fun.

Air Pressure

Pressure is the force acting on a certain area. For the same weight, pressure is more if the area on which the weight acts is small. Let us check this.

You will need:

- two shoulder bags, one with a wide strap and the other with a thin one
- heavy books

1. Load the bag with the wide strap, with the books.
2. Carry it on your shoulder for 2 minutes. Can you feel the pressure on your shoulder exerted by the weight of the books?
3. Transfer the books to the other bag and carry it in the same way for 2 minutes. Is there any difference in the pressure?

What makes the difference?

Find out

Why does a sharp knife cut better than a blunt one?

Atmospheric pressure

The atmosphere presses down on every square inch of the earth's surface with a weight of nearly 15 lbs, or on every square cm with a weight of 1 kg. It is this weight that we refer to when we talk of atmospheric pressure. Atmospheric pressure acts not only from above, but from all directions.

Air exerts pressure

You will need:

- a drinking glass
- water
- a piece of cardboard

1. Hold the glass over a sink and fill it to the brim with water.
2. Place the cardboard over it.
3. Hold the cardboard against the glass and turn the glass upside down.
4. Take away the hand holding the card. What happens? The air pushes against the card from below and keeps the water in the glass. The pressure of the air acting upwards is greater than the downward pressure of the water.

Remote-controlled water jet

You will need:

- a tin can
- a nail
- water

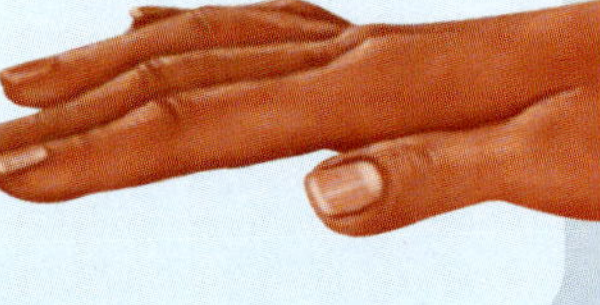

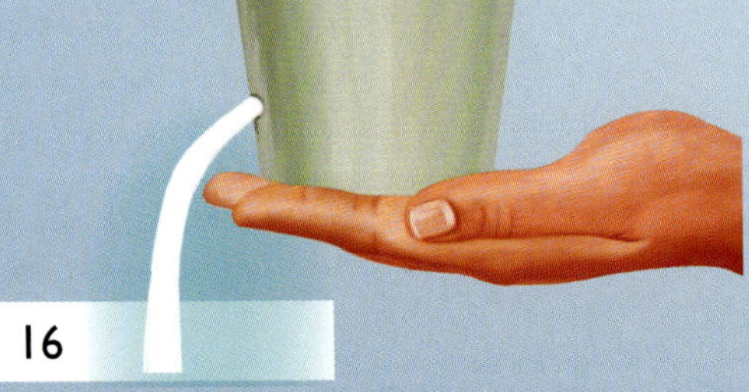

1. Make a hole with the nail near the bottom of the can.
2. Fill the can with water and hold it over a sink – water will gush out from the hole.
3. Hold your palm tightly over the top of the can so as to fully cover its mouth. Does the water stop running? By alternately pressing and removing your hand, you can control the water jet.

Make a siphon

You will need:

- two buckets/jars
- a plastic tube
- water
- a table/stand

1. The two containers should be half full of water. Place one container on the stand and the other on the ground.
2. Hold the plastic tube in a tub of water until it fills with water.
3. Pinch both the ends of the tube and put one end under water in each container. What do you observe? The air pressing down on the water in the container kept on the stand will force the water up the tube and down into the container kept below.
4. Vary the position of the container kept below and see the effect.

   What happens when the two containers are at the same level?

Nature equalises pressure

You will need:

- a shelled boiled egg
- a milk bottle
- newspaper
- a stick
- matches

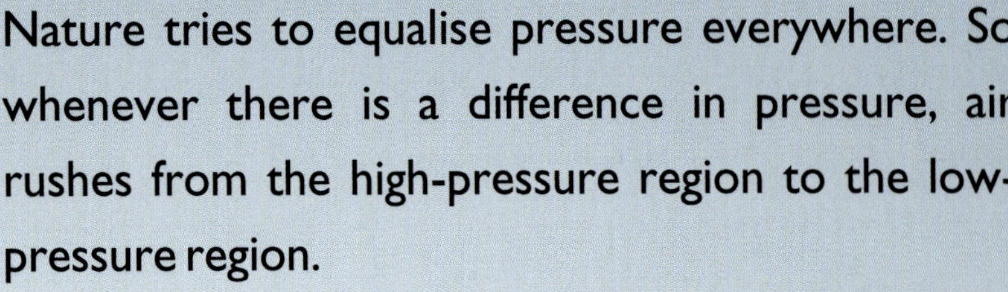

Nature tries to equalise pressure everywhere. So whenever there is a difference in pressure, air rushes from the high-pressure region to the low-pressure region.

1. Clean out and dry the milk bottle which has a neck slightly smaller than an egg.
2. Drop some crumpled paper inside the bottle and light it with the taper.
3. Stand the bottle upright. Place the egg at the mouth of the bottle and push.

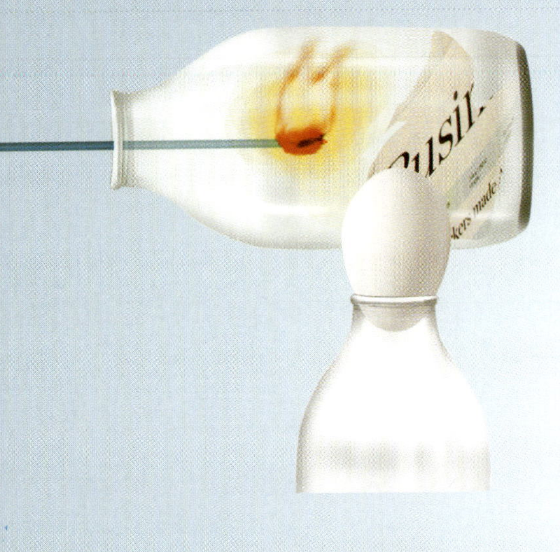

The bottle will greedily start to swallow the whole egg! After a while, the paper will stop burning. And soon the egg will stop moving. Can you say how this happens?

The trick works because of air pressure. As the paper burns, it uses up the oxygen in the bottle. So the pressure inside falls, and the outside pressure pushes the egg down. When the paper stops burning, the pressure inside does not fall any further and the egg stops moving.

Find out

How does a vacuum cleaner work?
When you switch on the cleaner, a fan reduces the pressure inside the machine. So air rushes in, carrying with it the dirt on the floor.

The Magdeburg Hemisphere

In 1654, Otto Von Guericke, a German scientist, performed an experiment to demonstrate the power of air pressure.

He used two iron hemispheres, each of which was about 22 inches in diameter. Their rims were smoothened and fitted together. He then pumped out the air from the hollow sphere. So great was the outside air pressure on the hemispheres, that it took 16 horses on each side to pull them apart!

You can perform a similar experiment with two plumber's force cups.

1. Wet the rims of two plumber's force cups.
2. Press the rubber cups tightly together and then try to separate them.

What holds the two cups together with such force?

Airlift

You have already found out how powerful air pressure can be.

Try this trick on your friends.

You will need:

- a balloon
- a plastic mug or beaker

1. Ask your friends if they can lift the beaker without touching it. All they can use is a balloon.
2. When your friends give up, just put the balloon inside the beaker and inflate it. You will find that the balloon will grip the beaker tightly due to the compressed air inside it. Now simply hold the balloon and lift the beaker up.

A balloon rocket

You will need:

- a balloon
- a straw
- scotch tape
- a pair of scissors
- twine
- a friend

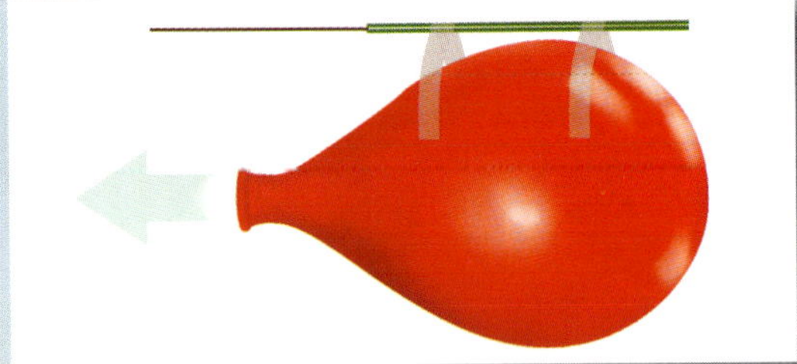

1. Cut a straw in half and pass the twine through it.
2. Tie the twine tightly across the room.
3. Blow the balloon and ask your friend to tape it to the straw while you hold the neck so that air cannot escape.
4. Blow some more air into the balloon and let it go. What happens? When the compressed air inside the balloon rushes out, it pushes the balloon in the opposite direction and the balloon moves. This principle is used in jet planes.

Hovercraft

A hovercraft is a vehicle that can move over both land and water. It has no wheels. Powerful fans blow air under the craft, which increase the air pressure. The high pressure pushes the hovercraft off the ground or water, so it floats on a cushion of compressed air.

Make your own hovercraft

You will need:

- a plastic box
- a pair of scissors
- a balloon

1. Make a hole in the centre of the plastic box with your scissors and push the neck of the balloon through the hole. Blow up the balloon, but do not tie the neck.
2. Put the box upside down on the table and give it a little push. The air in the inflated balloon will form a cushion inside the box and try to escape from the edges. This will reduce the friction between the table and the box, and it will glide along.

Moving Air

We can feel air if it is moving. Place your palm close to your mouth and blow on it. Can you feel the air flowing out of your mouth?

Switch the fan on, and immediately you will notice the movement of air in the room – your hair will fly, the curtains will sway, and you will feel cooler.

Move out of the room and try to locate any sign of the air moving – leaves moving on trees, clouds moving in the sky.

To study the effect of moving air, let us start with an easy experiment.

You will need:

- 2 ping-pong balls
- 2 metres of thread
- glue

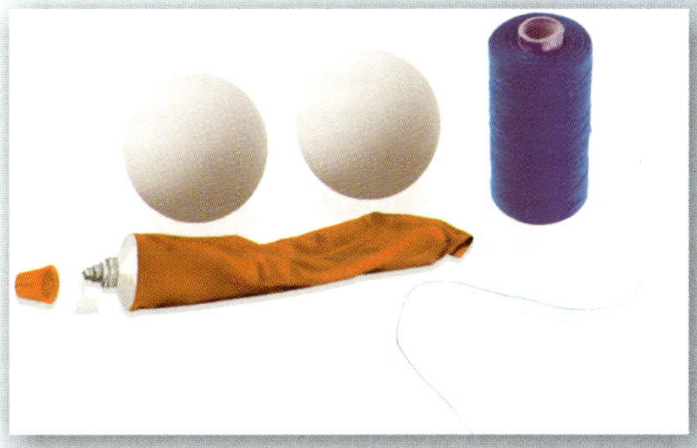

1. Cut the thread in half and glue an end of each part to the balls.
2. Hang the balls close together, about 10-12 centimetres apart, so that they are at the same level.
3. Try to separate the balls by blowing a steady stream of air between them. You will find that the harder you try, the closer the friendly balls will come. Why does this happen?

We owe the explanation to a Swiss scientist, Daniel Bernoulli, who, 200 years ago, found out that *a flowing liquid or gas lowers the barometric pressure of the area it occupies;* the faster it flows, the lower is the pressure. As Bernoulli's principle is true for all fluids flowing with moderate velocities, it is also true for air streams. So we can say that when air is moving, the air pressure is less

where the velocity of the stream is high, and the pressure is more where the velocity is low. That is why, by blowing air between the ping-pong balls in the experiment, you reduced the air pressure between them. The higher, normal air pressure surrounding the balls on the other sides pushed the balls towards each other, leaving you puzzled at their growing friendship!

Funnel fun

You will need:

- a funnel (it is best if you can get a transparent one)
- a ping-pong ball

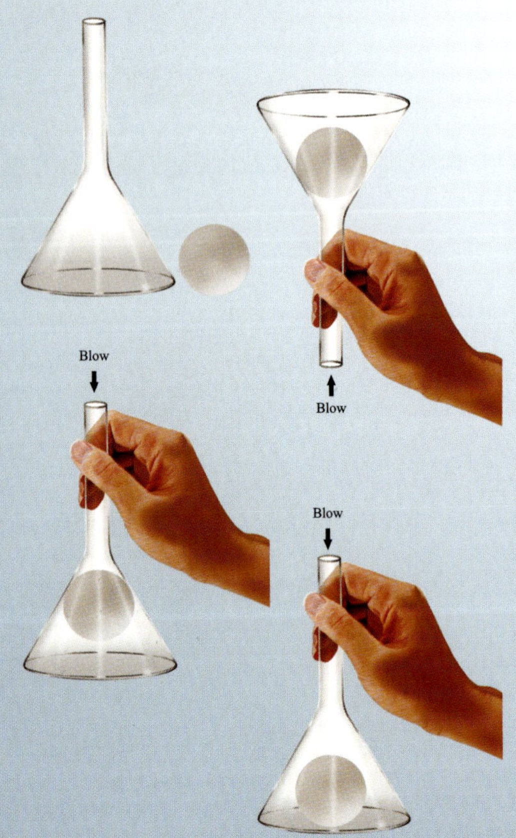

1. Put the ball inside the funnel.
2. Blow hard through the stem of the funnel and see if you can blow the ball out of the funnel. Apply Bernoulli's principle to explain the behaviour of the ping-pong ball.
3. Invert the funnel and hold the ball in the cup.
4. Blow hard through the stem and remove the hand holding the ball. What happens? Who holds the ball?
5. Place the ball on the table and cover it with the funnel.
6. Now blow through the stem. Can you lift the ball off the table?

An anti-gravity card

You will need:

- a big spool of thread
- a thumbtack
- a card

1. Join the diagonals to get the centre of the card.
2. Stick the thumbtack at the centre.
3. Bring the spool near your mouth, so that it points towards the ground.
4. Gently press the card to the other end of the spool, so that the pin is in the hole of the spool, and blow.
5. Now remove your finger. The card defies gravity and sticks to your spool! By now you surely know that the air stream just below the card lowered the pressure on the card, and the surrounding air held it to the spool.

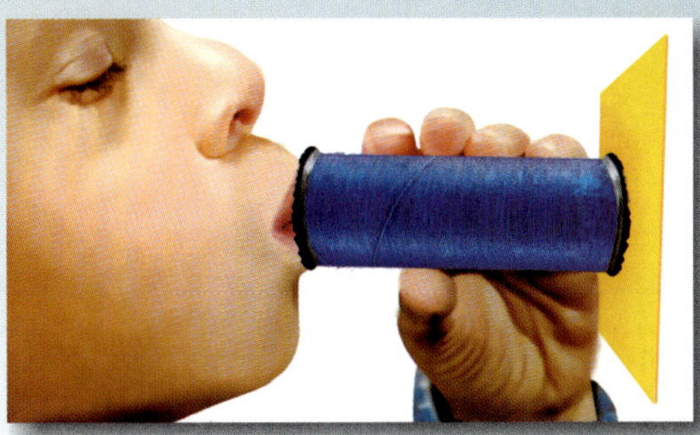

Blow the bridge

Ask your friends how good their lung power is. Can they blow off a paper bridge? If they laugh at you, just ask them to try this.

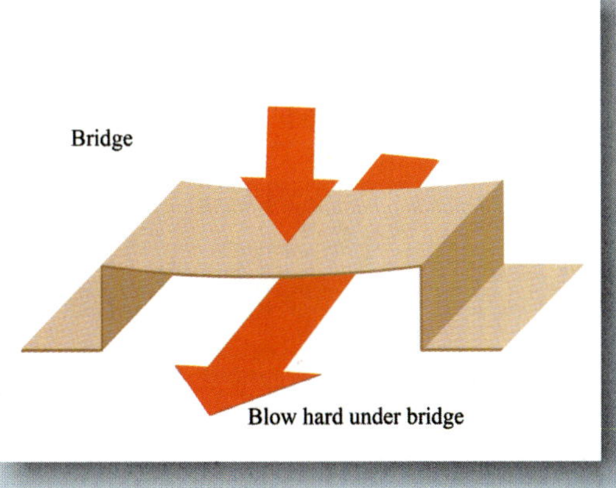

1. Make a bridge out of a 20 cm × 10 cm thin cardboard piece. Bend it about 2 cm on each end and place it on the table.
2. Ask your friends to take turns and try blowing the bridge by blowing air through the arch.

   The harder they try, the greater will be the force holding it to the table.

Make a spray-gun

1. Get two glass tubes.
2. Hold one of the tubes in a glass of coloured water and hold the other at a right angle to the first one so that the ends of the two tubes are close together.
3. Blow through the horizontal tube. What happens to the water level in the vertical tube?

The air jet at the junction of the tubes reduces the air pressure at that point and the atmospheric pressure pushes the liquid up the tube, which then gets sprayed with the air stream. This is how a perfume sprayer works.

Wind

When air moves from one place to another, we get wind. The speed and direction of wind depends on the air pressure and temperature. Winds are caused by warm, light air rising, and cooler, denser air moving in to take its place.

Make a waver

You will need:

- 4 sheets of coloured crepe or tissue paper
- a colourful 8"×2" sheet of wrapping paper
- a straw and a pair of scissors

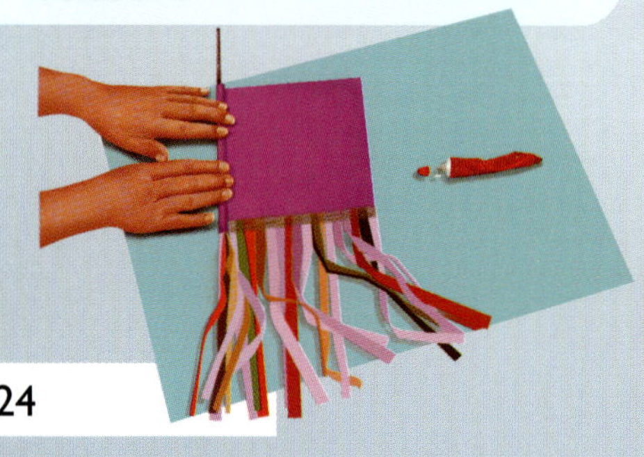

1. Cut some strips of coloured tissue paper.
2. Glue the streamers along the bottom of the wrapping paper.
3. Place the straw on one side of the paper and roll it into a colourful handle. Glue the end and leave it to dry.
4. Take your waver outside to check if there is any breeze. Run with the waver and watch the streamers lift in the air.

Make a wind-vane

A wind-vane is used to tell the direction of wind.

You will need:

- a strong card
- a pencil
- a pair of scissors
- plastic drinking straws
- glue
- a tall plastic bottle
- sand
- a long thin rod
- a rubber band
- a compass needle

1. Draw a wind-vane on the card. Cut it out.
2. Glue a straw to the centre of the vane.
3. Fix the pencil at right angles to the rod with the rubber band, so that it forms a cross.
4. Fill the bottle with sand, and stick the rod into the sand.
5. Write N on a square piece of card and stick it to the pencil.
6. Place a small piece of drinking straw on the rod so that it rests on the crossbar.
7. Place the wind-vane on the rod. It should turn freely.
8. Take your wind-vane outside. With the help of the compass, find out which way North is. Position your wind-vane so that N points towards North. The direction of the vane will give you the direction of the wind.

Find out

Paint a picture of a weather cock in bright colours and replace the vane with it. Put it up on top of a building and observe.

Make an anemometer

An anemometer measures the speed of wind.

You will need:

- 4 empty ice cream cups
- paper and glue
- red and green paint and a brush
- 3 thin, 25 cm long wooden sticks
- a tall plastic bottle filled with sand
- a cork, a round bead and a pin

1. Cover the ice cream cups with paper. Paint three cups green and one cup red.
2. Glue two sticks at right angles and secure them with the pin. Glue the cups in a clockwise direction to the four ends of the sticks.
3. Glue the cork to the third stick and put it in the bottle.
4. Place the bead on the cork. Push the pin down. Check if the cups turn freely.
5. Put your anemometer outside. To have a rough estimate of the wind speed, count the number of complete turns the red cup makes in 30 seconds. Divide this number by 10 to get the wind speed in kms/hr.

Make a windsock

You will need:

- an old shirt sleeve
- a wire loop and twine
- a long stick or pole and a nail

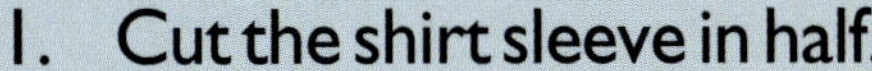

1. Cut the shirt sleeve in half.
2. Sew one end of the sleeve to the wire loop.
3. Tie a piece of twine to the loop.
4. Fix a nail on the pole and tie the twine to this nail.
5. Tie a few more pieces of twine around the loop in this manner.
6. Now, mount your windsock outside. It will give you an idea of the strength and direction of the wind.

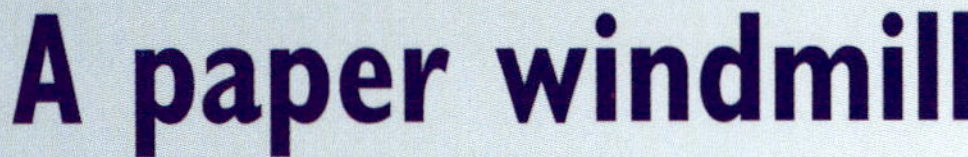

A paper windmill

You will need:

- a square sheet of coloured marble paper
- plastic drinking straws
- a short length of wire
- a pair of scissors
- some glue
- a wind-vane stand

1. Fold along the diagonals of the square, then press and open the sheet.
2. Cut half-way along each diagonal towards the centre.
3. Fold over alternate loose ends and fix at the centre with some glue.
4. Pierce a small hole at the centre.
5. Bend one end of the wire. Through the other end, first pass the windmill, then a short piece of straw and finally pierce it through one end of a straw.
6. Now bend this end of the wire so that the windmill is held firm. At the same time, it should turn freely.
7. Place your windmill on the wind-vane stand and put it out in the wind.

Flight and Flotation

If you drop a ball and a stone from the same height, they reach the ground at the same time. This is true for all bodies, since the same acceleration, the acceleration due to gravity, is acting on all of them. This was proved by the great Italian scientist Galileo Galilei. But what happens if you drop a small piece of paper or a feather along with the ball?

Even before you do the experiment, you know that the feather and the paper will take a much longer time to reach the ground. In other words, they will float in the air. Any object will float in the air if it is lighter than the volume of air it is displacing.

Have you then proved Galileo wrong? No, not really, because if there was no air to support the paper and the feather, they would indeed reach the ground at the same time as the ball and the stone.

How long does a balloon float?

1. Blow a balloon. Tie a thread around its neck.
2. Lift the balloon and leave it. You will find that it slowly comes down and will need a periodic upward push to keep it afloat. Then how do the advertisement balloons float? These balloons are filled with helium or hydrogen gas which is lighter than air.

Flying

Man has always had a desire to fly. In order to fly, you need two things – something to lift you up in the air and keep you afloat, and secondly, a force to make you move ahead in the air. Wings provide the necessary lift to flying objects.

Airlift

1. Take a strip of paper 30 cms long and 5 cms wide.
2. Fold the paper about 5 cms from one end. Crease the fold well.
3. Now hold the short end of the fold against your chin and blow hard across the top surface of the paper. The stream of air will lower the pressure on the top surface of the paper and air from below will push it up.

Wings act in a similar way. A wing is a special shape called an *aerofoil*. Birds have very powerful chest muscles to flap their wings up and down. As a bird's wings beat downwards, they create more air pressure under the wings. This extra pressure pushes the bird upwards. Insects also have very thin flat wings with powerful muscles. Both insects and birds have very light bodies. This helps them to keep afloat.

Make a wing

1. Cut a strip of paper about 30 cms long and 5 cms wide.
2. Bend and tape the ends as shown to form a wing.
3. Punch two holes in the wing and pass a short length of straw in place.
4. Push a piece of twine down the straw.
5. Hold the thread at the two ends and blow on the leading edge of the aerofoil. What do you observe? The wing will experience a lift due to the difference in air pressure caused by the air stream.

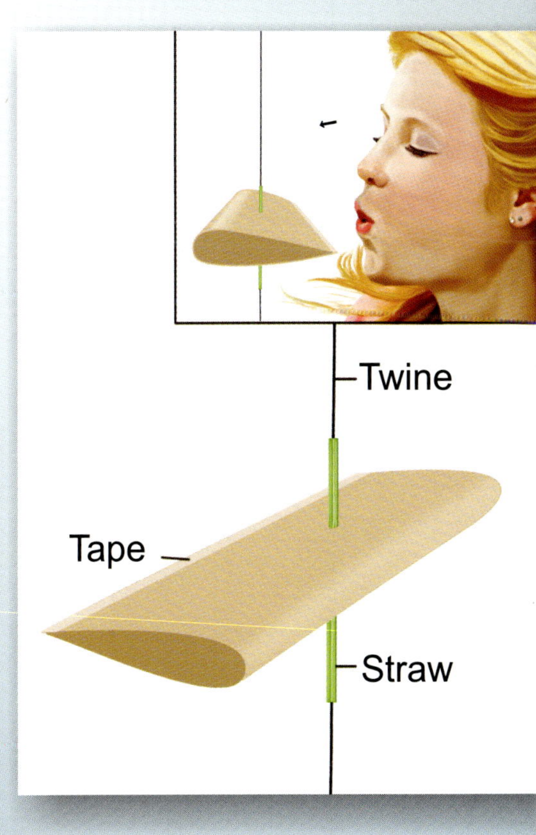

What provides this air stream to lift flying things off the ground?

Did you know that flies can beat their wings as fast as 1,000 times a second?

Aeroplanes do not flap their wings. To take off, a plane uses its engines to move fast along the runway. As it moves, air flows over its wings and produces the lift. When there is enough lift to overcome the force of gravity, the plane takes off.

A paper glider

1. Fold an A4-size paper in half along the longer side. Open it out.
2. Fold the top corners inwards so that they meet in the middle.
3. Fold the corners once more.
4. Turn the paper over.
5. Fold the sides inwards to the middle.
6. Fold the glider outwards in half. You should be able to see three folds.
7. Grip the central fold and flatten the side ones. These are the wings of the glider.
8. Glue the wings together under the belly.
9. Fix a paper clip to the nose of the glider. Fly the glider. Does the paper clip help it fly?
10. Cut some small flaps in the end of the wings. Bend the flaps up and down and see how you can manoeuvre its flight.

What is common between your glider, a bird and an aeroplane?

The five exhibitions underpinning ROTOR III & IV reflected a diversity of disciplines, practices and curatorial strategies, and formed the nucleus of a much wider set of activities and events that constituted the programme. As part of its multi-layered engagement strategy, for example, ROTOR III & IV embarked upon an innovative and fruitful collaboration with Turvey World Dance, establishing a series of workshops and performances which ran in parallel with each exhibition. These sought to approach exhibition interpretation in a multi-sensory and non-prescriptive manner, with a view to overcoming some of the barriers to understanding and enjoying contemporary visual culture. Other engagement techniques which signalled a development from ROTOR I & II included the implementation of what might be considered '360 degree' engagement, whereby visitors were encouraged, during workshops and through the exhibition's creative feedback mechanisms, to enter into dialogue with the artists and with other visitors, to propose to the artists the sorts of questions they wished to ask of them; effectively holding a mirror up to its curatorial, exhibitionary and art-viewing processes. For the *Open House* exhibition, in the spirit of co-production fundamental to its conceptual identity, visitors were invited to collaborate with the artists and with the work, participating in the creation of exhibition content through ongoing opportunities for interaction and dialogue. Surpassing ROTOR I & II in terms of audience figures, engaging a total of 28,149 visitors to its exhibitions (an average of 74 per day) and over 5000 participants in its accompanying events and activities, was an achievement heightened by the challenging circumstances within which it was operating.

Image courtesy of Jamie Collier

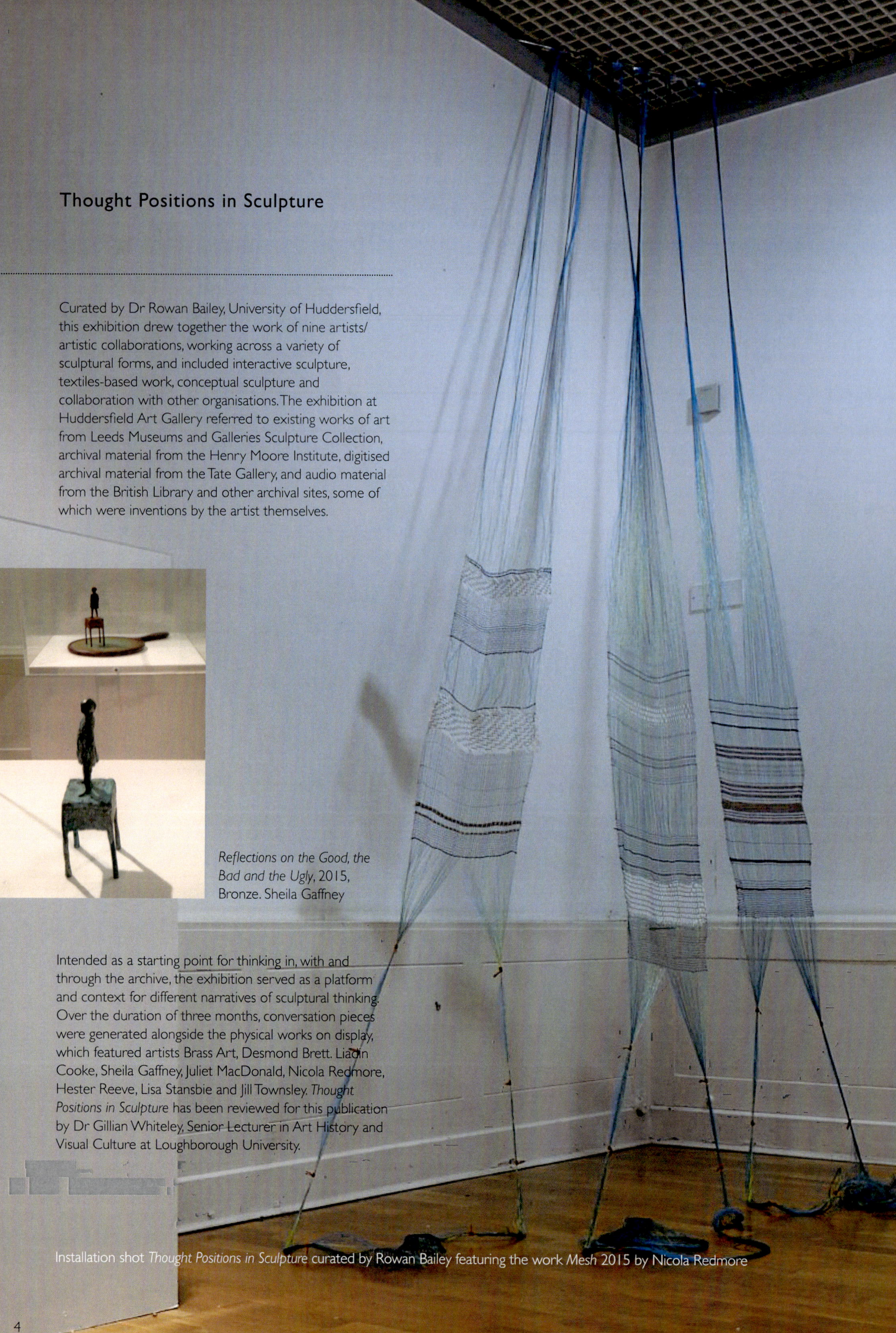

Thought Positions in Sculpture

Curated by Dr Rowan Bailey, University of Huddersfield, this exhibition drew together the work of nine artists/ artistic collaborations, working across a variety of sculptural forms, and included interactive sculpture, textiles-based work, conceptual sculpture and collaboration with other organisations. The exhibition at Huddersfield Art Gallery referred to existing works of art from Leeds Museums and Galleries Sculpture Collection, archival material from the Henry Moore Institute, digitised archival material from the Tate Gallery, and audio material from the British Library and other archival sites, some of which were inventions by the artist themselves.

Reflections on the Good, the Bad and the Ugly, 2015, Bronze. Sheila Gaffney

Intended as a starting point for thinking in, with and through the archive, the exhibition served as a platform and context for different narratives of sculptural thinking. Over the duration of three months, conversation pieces were generated alongside the physical works on display, which featured artists Brass Art, Desmond Brett. Liadin Cooke, Sheila Gaffney, Juliet MacDonald, Nicola Redmore, Hester Reeve, Lisa Stansbie and Jill Townsley. *Thought Positions in Sculpture* has been reviewed for this publication by Dr Gillian Whiteley, Senior Lecturer in Art History and Visual Culture at Loughborough University.

Installation shot *Thought Positions in Sculpture* curated by Rowan Bailey featuring the work *Mesh* 2015 by Nicola Redmore

China East-West: The Alternative Face of Globalisation in Urban and Rural Transformations

Curated by Professor Nicholas Temple, Dr Yun Gao and Dr Ioanni Delsante, colleagues in the architecture faculty at University of Huddersfield, this exhibition provided a 'window' into the dramatic changes taking place in Chinese urban and rural life. Exploring urban design in China through photographs, drawings, architectural models, maps and films, this architectural exhibition explored the changing face of regional urbanism and posed questions about how the environmental, economic and social challenges facing many parts of the world might provide opportunities for regional cities and towns in the North of England to develop alternative forms of urban living, which are fundamentally different from those of the rapidly expanding metropolises. It featured student as well as staff research, and students from both MA and undergraduate architecture courses were involved in supporting its engagement activities. *China East-West* has been reviewed by Luigi Stenardo, Associate Professor of Civil, Environmental and Architectural Engineering at Università di Padova, Italy.

Installation shot *China East-West* curated by Professor Nicholas Temple, Dr Yun Gao and Dr Ioanni Delsante

Open House: A Collaboration of Experts

Curated by Lydia Catterall, this exhibition signalled a new partnership between ROTOЯ and Leeds-based East Street Arts. It embedded public engagement at its heart through opportunities for interaction, working in a responsive manner to feedback as it was received, and focusing on Huddersfield and its people, as both a rich archive and motif to initiate a co-produced public exhibition. Remaining true to the 'transdisciplinary dialogue and debate' ethos that ran through ROTOЯ, the exhibition incorporated public workshops and artist residencies, forming a vibrant, open working space in which discussion was able to develop. It invited proposals from regional artists interested in working with local people, places and archives to respond, through exhibition content, to ideas around site, memory and community.

The selected artists – David Armes, Jim Bond, Liz Walker, Rozi Fuller, ReetSo and Nicola Golightly – had access to space within Huddersfield Art Gallery, which they used as their primary studio space during an initial four-week residency period. At the start of this four-week residency period, a 'skeletal' exhibition from the existing Huddersfield Art Gallery and Kirklees museum archives and collections, selected by each artist via early conversations with their community and with Gallery staff, formed an initial backdrop to the opening of the exhibition and acted at a starting point for conversations with visitors, which, in turn, fed into the production of new works of art. For this publication, *Open House* was reviewed by artist Gemma Lacey.

Installation shot *Open House: A Collaboration of Experts* exhibition curated by Lydia Catterall featuring the work of David Armes

Migrations

Curated by Professor Jessica Hemmings, now of University of Gothenburg, Sweden, *Migrations* explored the notion of textiles as carriers of multiple cultural influences put forth in the accompanying publication, Cultural Threads: transnational textiles today[1], *Migrations* examined the ways in which cloth and fabric can act as cultural markers, their portability meaning that they will often travel with people around the globe. The exhibition also addressed the hybrid position of textiles within the worlds of craft, design and art. It featured as part of an international tour which included America, Ireland and Australia. The ROTOЯ exhibition made connections with Huddersfield's rich textiles heritage and Yorkshire's Year of the Textile, and it incorporated poetry-in-residence as well as targeted outreach workshops with local schools through collaboration with The Children's Art School, in addition to artist and curator talks, interactive, tactile interpretation methods, and Turvey World dance workshops and performances. *Migrations* was reviewed for this publication by Dr Christine Checinska, Associate Research Fellow at the University of Johannesburg and writer, designer, curator and dancer, who writes about textiles, culture and race.

Toril Johannessen, *Unlearning Optical Illusions I-IV*, 2014-18
Printed textiles

Discursive Documents

Curated by Dr Liam Devlin, University of Huddersfield, *Discursive Documents* further expanded on the dialogic element of ROTOЯ and its desire to communicate and connect effectively with its publics. It did so by exploring the photograph's potential to prompt debate, not necessarily to address 'how things are' but to ask 'what is possible'. It looked at how photographs act as both a document (of events or moments) and as an artistic/aesthetic image. Featuring the work of several key photographers, the exhibition addressed themes including migration and the body and invited visitors to situate themselves between the images to consider, question and debate the themes they explored; becoming a part of the dialogue between them. The exhibitions paired artists and photographers whose work could be linked thematically. Seba Kurtis's seductive and fragile images from Calais were set in relation to Alex Beldea's portraits and appropriated images from refugees fleeing the conflict in the Middle East. The everyday assumptions that we bring to photographs when we 'read' or try to understand them are challenged by both Richard Mulhearn and Richard Higginbottom's deliberately ambiguous images. Mulhearn's images celebrate those moments when we subconsciously slip out of the conventional behaviour expected of us; while Higginbottom's work is a response to cultural theorist Michel De Certeau's exploration of the complexity of the modern city, which he described as a 'swarming mass of innumerable singularities' (de Certeau 1984: 97). Finally, Layla Sailor and Sarah Eyre's work used collages and gifs to disrupt the flow of clichéd images of female bodies, and to explore the boundaries between objects and bodies. *Discursive Documents* was reviewed for this publication by Anna Taylor, artist and editor of *Backburner Journal*.

Layla Sailor, *Dolores II*, 2017
Digital Duraclear Print. Image courtesy of Silvana Trevale

Satellite exhibitions and projects

As part of ROTOЯ's commitment to making its exhibitions relevant and interesting to a varied audience, a further satellite exhibition was developed in collaboration with the School of Education and curator Olaojo Aiyegbayo. The exhibition showcased a series of historical British political newspaper cartoons depicting issues relating to race and ethnicity from the 1950s to early 2000s. Satirising racism, discrimination and immigration – issues with significant contemporary resonance – the exhibition was held across two sites within the University campus and enabled a new generation of students, staff and members of the public to experience the ways in which political satire can stimulate positive conversations around the importance of making equality, diversity and sanctuary a fundamental part of British culture.

A series of fringe events and activities supported ROTOЯ III & IV's continuing commitment to making all forms of art and design accessible, relatable and interesting to as many people as possible, while also aiming to communicate widely the ethos and ideas which underpinned the programme. These included events outside of conventional gallery spaces, such as a pop-up exhibition and young people's workshop in Leeds for its Unity Day festival, collaborations with the Children's Art School, Holmfirth[2], and workshops at the 2017 Engage Conference, Bristol. The latter acted primarily as a means of disseminating a newly developed toolkit – a collaboration between ROTOЯ and Fun Palaces who are an ongoing campaign for cultural democracy[3]. The toolkit, which was piloted at the conference, was designed as a free, downloadable resource to support those wishing to work collaboratively to develop public-facing arts events and activities, by prompting questions, suggesting possibilities acting as an ice-breaker tool for groups working together for the first time. Positively received at the conference, it presented ROTOЯ as an exemplar and model for ways of exploring the provision of cost-effective cultural services within a locale.

Image courtesy of Silvana Trevale

Presenting the insights of ROTOЯ

ROTOЯ III & IV expanded its scope in a research context, working in a cross-disciplinary manner to connect with other research projects happening across the University. It had a presence at the 2017 Researchers' Night at the University, which saw young people from across the UK exploring the programme and participating in activities that sought to broaden understanding of, and share learning from the programme. ROTOЯ further inaugurated its own evolution as a form of action-research, in which its approaches to exhibition design and delivery acted as a self-reflexive mechanism for assimilating learning back into the programme, as well as communicating it externally. The effect of this was a responsive programme in which cumulative changes were trialled around its engagement, interpretation, marketing and dissemination methods as each exhibition progressed.

Marking the culmination of the two phases of ROTOЯ and its 13 exhibitions, and to continue dialogue and learning around the ways in which partnership working and cultural leadership might be used to reinterpret and rejuvenate a place's cultural offer, a ROTOЯ conference entitled Culture, Community, Creativity was held in January 2018 at the Lawrence Batley theatre in Huddersfield. As well as disseminating and celebrating the programme's outcomes, the conference also positioned our goal of exploring new challenges and possibilities for an art and design programme in the region. The speakers, panelists and workshop facilitators at Culture, Community, Creativity were invited from a range of backgrounds and from across a breadth of specialisms, and included academics, professionals and individuals representing organisations, from across the arts and cultural sector both in the UK and internationally.

The questions and provocations which underpinned Culture, Community, Creativity and which were opened up to participants for further discussion were those to which ROTOЯ had aimed to respond through its exhibitions and events, and those which emerged from the programme, at times as unexpected outcomes. They were recognised, through having worked with a range of stakeholders, as being transferable to a breadth of projects, practitioners, organisations and institutions both locally and further afield. ROTOЯ, then, was positioned simply as the starting point or catalyst for what was a series of engaging discussions around the challenges and benefits of projects which aim to achieve one of ROTOЯ's key visions – of exploring how we create the conditions for creative thinking and action to flourish. These discussions had an emphasis on the intersections of the arts, people and places, and asked participants

Installation shot *Open House: A Collaborative of Experts* exhibition curated by Lydia Catterall featuring an outcome from the ReetSo public workshop.